P9-CMO-556

Voyages

also edited by Lee Bennett Hopkins

RAINBOWS ARE MADE: Poems by Carl Sandburg

VOYAGES

POEMS BY

WALT WHITMAN

Selected by
LEE BENNETT HOPKINS

With illustrations by
CHARLES MIKOLAYCAK

Harcourt Brace Jovanovich, Publishers

SAN DIEGO   NEW YORK   LONDON

NORTHPORT PUBLIC LIBRARY
NORTHPORT, NEW YORK

Introduction and compilation copyright © 1988 by Lee Bennett Hopkins
Illustrations copyright © 1988 by Charles Mikolaycak

All rights reserved. No part of this publication may be reproduced
or transmitted in any form or by any means, electronic or mechanical,
including photocopy, recording, or any information storage and
retrieval system, without permission in writing from the publisher.

Requests for permission to make copies of any part of the work should
be mailed to: Permissions, Harcourt Brace Jovanovich, Publishers,
Orlando, Florida 32887.

LIBRARY OF CONGRESS CATALOGING IN PUBLICATION DATA

Whitman, Walt, 1819–1892.
Voyages.

Includes indexes.
Summary: A collection of fifty-three poems and
selections from poems focusing on the people and
places encountered by the nineteenth-century American
writer from his mid-thirties through his early seventies.
[1. American poetry]   I. Hopkins, Lee Bennett.
II. Mikolaycak, Charles, ill.   III. Title.
PS3204.H66   1988   811'.3   87-33353
ISBN 0-15-294495-8

Designed by Gracie Artemis
Printed in the United States of America
First edition
A   B   C   D   E   F

To
ANNA BIER
and
CHARLES MIKOLAYCAK
who made this voyage possible
and
to
WALT WHITMAN
who will forever travel it
—LBH

To
LEE BENNETT HOPKINS,
the Bull's Head Theater, and Trenton
—CM

CONTENTS

"*I mourned, and yet shall mourn . . .*"

"*I am the poet of the Body and I am the poet of the Soul . . .*"

"So long—*And I hope we shall meet again.*"

INTRODUCTION

On May 7, 1984, Walt Whitman became one of the first writers to be admitted to the American Poets' Corner, which is housed in the cathedral church of St. John the Divine in New York City. Today, well over a century after Walt Whitman's *Leaves of Grass* was published (1855), his works appear in major anthologies throughout the world. Countless biographies have been written about him; endless numbers of critiques, essays, papers flow from pens; they will continue, for his fascinating life and work changed the course of American literature forever, speaking to and influencing generations of readers and writers through his emotionally charged verse.

He was a nineteenth-century rebel—caring, daring, sharing, undaunted by reviews and the opinions of major literary voices, family, or friends. He wrote from deep within himself, speaking of the many places and faces he encountered. His voyages took him from Paumanok (Long Island, New York) to his beloved Mannahatta (New York City), and then to America's North, South, East, and West; he spent time in Ohio, Illinois, Kentucky, Washington, D.C., Louisiana, and New Jersey.

Walt Whitman was an "I" poet, setting down commanding statements about self: "I celebrate myself, and sing myself . . ."; "I am the poet of the Body and I am the poet of the Soul. . . . I am the poet of the woman the same as the man." But Walt Whitman's "I" was the "I" of all people.

"Whitman is America," said Ezra Pound. William Carlos Williams called him *the* "pioneer of American poetry." Langston Hughes stated: ". . . his poems contain us all. The reader cannot help but see his own better self therein." Louis Untermeyer commented that he is "unquestionably the most challenging writer of his time and of ours."

Walter Whitman, Jr., was born on May 31, 1819, at West Hills, Huntington, Long Island, New York, to poor, obscure parents of English, Dutch, and Welsh descent— the second son in a family of nine children.

When he was four years old, his parents moved to Brooklyn, New York. At twelve, one year after leaving school, he became a printer's apprentice and worked at learning the newspaper trade during his teens. In his early twenties and thirties, he held several jobs, including editing two Brooklyn newspapers and doing some carpentry with his father, in between restlessly roaming and writing.

Leaves of Grass appeared when he was thirty-six years old; it contained twelve untitled poems and a preface. It was the beginning of a work that would go through varied editions throughout his entire life, ending with the ninth revision known as the "death-bed" edition, containing 438 pages, published in 1892, the year of his death.

Upon reading the first edition of *Leaves of Grass*, Ralph Waldo Emerson, a contemporary of Whitman and one of the few to recognize the book's greatness and impact, wrote him a letter stating: "I find it the most extraordinary piece of wit and wisdom that America has yet contributed. . . . I greet you at the beginning of a great career."

Whitman made little money from the book's sales, returning to editorial work until the Civil War, during which time he spent a great many of his waking hours as a wound-dresser for soldiers in Washington, D.C., hospitals.

In 1873, he suffered a paralytic stroke from which he never fully recovered and moved to Camden, New Jersey. In 1884, he bought a shabby, noise-ridden slum dwelling at 328 Mickle Street, where he died on March 26, 1892, two months before his seventy-third birthday. His home in Camden is now open to visitors, thanks to the Walt Whitman Association and the State of New Jersey.

Voyages contains fifty-three selections, divided into five sections, written by Walt Whitman between his mid-thirties and his early seventies. The sections encompass the poet's views of his youth, his strong sense of self, vivid thoughts about his various journeys, a profound depiction of war, death, and mourning, his portraits of people whom he had met, and, finally, his musings about old age and coming to terms with death.

In the third edition of *Leaves of Grass* (1860), Walt Whitman included "Salut au Monde!" Part one of the piece reads:

O take my hand Walt Whitman!
Such gliding wonders! such sights and sounds!
Such join'd unended links, each hook'd to the next,
Each answering all, each sharing the earth with all.

What widens within you Walt Whitman?
What waves and soils exuding?
What climes? what persons and cities are here?
Who are the infants, some playing, some slumbering?
Who are the girls? who are the married women?
Who are the groups of old men going slowly with their arms
    about each other's necks?
What rivers are these? what forests and fruits are these?
What are the mountains call'd that rise so high in the mists?
What myriads of dwellings are they fill'd with dwellers?

Join me in taking this master poet's hand. Enter *his* voyages. Find what widens within *you*—and within this man.

LEE BENNETT HOPKINS
Scarborough, New York

"Out of the cradle endlessly rocking . . ."

SHUT NOT YOUR DOORS

Shut not your doors to me proud libraries,
For that which was lacking on all your well-fill'd shelves, yet
    needed most, I bring,
Forth from the war emerging, a book I have made,
The words of my book nothing, the drift of it every thing,
A book separate, not link'd with the rest nor felt by the
    intellect,
But you ye untold latencies will thrill to every page.

THOU READER

Thou reader throbbest life and pride and love the same as I,
Therefore for thee the following chants.

From

SONG OF MYSELF

I celebrate myself, and sing myself,
And what I assume you shall assume,
For every atom belonging to me as good belongs to you.

I loafe and invite my soul,
I lean and loafe at my ease observing a spear of summer
   grass.

My tongue, every atom of my blood, form'd from this soil,
   this air,
Born here of parents born here from parents the same, and
   their parents the same,
I, now thirty-seven years old in perfect health begin,
Hoping to cease not till death.

From

STARTING FROM PAUMANOK

Starting from fish-shape Paumanok where I was born,
Well-begotten, and rais'd by a perfect mother,
After roaming many lands, lover of populous pavements,
Dweller in Mannahatta my city, or on southern savannas,
Or a soldier camp'd or carrying my knapsack and gun, or a
    miner in California,
Or rude in my home in Dakota's woods, my diet meat, my
    drink from the spring,
Or withdrawn to muse and meditate in some deep recess,
Far from the clank of crowds intervals passing rapt and
    happy,
Aware of the fresh free giver the flowing Missouri, aware of
    mighty Niagara,
Aware of the buffalo herds grazing the plains, the hirsute and
    strong-breasted bull,
Of earth, rocks, Fifth-month flowers experienced, stars,
    rain, snow, my amaze,
Having studied the mocking-bird's tones and the flight of
    the mountain-hawk,
And heard at dawn the unrivall'd one, the hermit thrush
    from the swamp-cedars,
Solitary, singing in the West, I strike up for a New World.

MANNAHATTA

I was asking for something specific and perfect for my city,
Whereupon lo! upsprang the aboriginal name.

Now I see what there is in a name, a word, liquid, sane,
    unruly, musical, self-sufficient,
I see that the word of my city is that word from of old,
Because I see that word nested in nests of water-bays,
    superb,
Rich, hemm'd thick all around with sailships and
    steamships, an island sixteen miles long, solid-founded,
Numberless crowded streets, high growths of iron, slender,
    strong, light, splendidly uprising toward clear skies,
Tides swift and ample, well-loved by me, toward sundown,
The flowing sea-currents, the little islands, larger adjoining
    islands, the heights, the villas,
The countless masts, the white shore-steamers, the
    lighters, the ferry-boats, the black sea-steamers
    well model'd,
The down-town streets, the jobbers' houses of business, the
    houses of business of the ship-merchants and
    money-brokers, the river-streets,
Immigrants arriving, fifteen or twenty thousand in a week,
The carts hauling goods, the manly race of drivers of
    horses, the brown-faced sailors,
The summer air, the bright sun shining, and the sailing
    clouds aloft,

The winter snows, the sleigh-bells, the broken ice in the
    river, passing along up or down with the flood-tide or
    ebb-tide,
The mechanics of the city, the masters, well form'd,
    beautiful-faced, looking you straight in the eyes,
Trottoirs throng'd, vehicles, Broadway, the women, the
    shops and shows,
A million people—manners free and superb—open voices—
    hospitality—the most courageous and friendly young men,
City of hurried and sparkling waters! city of spires and
    masts!
City nested in bays! my city!

I HEAR AMERICA SINGING

I hear America singing, the varied carols I hear,
Those of mechanics, each one singing his as it should be
    blithe and strong,
The carpenter singing his as he measures his plank or beam,
The mason singing his as he makes ready for work, or
    leaves off work,
The boatman singing what belongs to him in his boat, the
    deckhand singing on the steamboat deck,
The shoemaker singing as he sits on his bench, the hatter
    singing as he stands,
The wood-cutter's song, the ploughboy's on his way in the
    morning, or at noon intermission or at sundown,
The delicious singing of the mother, or of the young wife
    at work, or of the girl sewing or washing,
Each singing what belongs to him or her and to none else,
The day what belongs to the day—at night the party of
    young fellows, robust, friendly,
Singing with open mouths their strong melodious songs.

From

STARTING FROM PAUMANOK

See, steamers steaming through my poems,
See, in my poems immigrants continually coming and
   landing,
See, in arriere, the wigwam, the trail, the hunter's hut, the
   flat-boat, the maize-leaf, the claim, the rude fence, and
   the backwoods village,
See, on the one side the Western Sea and on the other the
   Eastern Sea, how they advance and retreat upon my poems
   as upon their own shores,
See, pastures and forests in my poems—see, animals wild
   and tame—see, beyond the Kaw, countless herds of
   buffalo feeding on short curly grass,
See, in my poems, cities, solid, vast, inland, with paved
   streets, with iron and stone edifices, ceaseless vehicles,
   and commerce,
See, the many-cylinder'd steam printing-press—see, the
   electric telegraph stretching across the continent,
See, through Atlantica's depths pulses American Europe
   reaching, pulses of Europe duly return'd,
See, the strong and quick locomotive as it departs, panting,
   blowing the steam-whistle,
See, ploughmen ploughing farms—see, miners digging
   mines—see, the numberless factories,
See, mechanics busy at their benches with tools—see from
   among them superior judges, philosophs, Presidents,
   emerge, drest in working dresses,
See, lounging through the shops and fields of the States,
   me well-belov'd, close-held by day and night,
Hear the loud echoes of my songs there—read the hints
   come at last.

A LEAF FOR HAND IN HAND

A leaf for hand in hand;
You natural persons old and young!
You on the Mississippi and on all the branches and bayous
  of the Mississippi!
You friendly boatmen and mechanics! you roughs!
You twain! and all processions moving along the streets!
I wish to infuse myself among you till I see it common for
  you to walk hand in hand.

OUT OF THE CRADLE
ENDLESSLY ROCKING

Out of the cradle endlessly rocking,
Out of the mocking-bird's throat, the musical shuttle,
Out of the Ninth-month midnight,
Over the sterile sands and the fields beyond, where the child
    leaving his bed wander'd alone, bareheaded, barefoot,
Down from the shower'd halo,
Up from the mystic play of shadows twining and twisting
    as if they were alive,
Out from the patches of briers and blackberries,
From the memories of the bird that chanted to me,
From your memories sad brother, from the fitful risings and
    fallings I heard,
From under that yellow half-moon late-risen and swollen
    as if with tears,
From those beginning notes of yearning and love there in
    the mist,
From the thousand responses of my heart never to cease,
From the myriad thence-arous'd words,

From the word stronger and more delicious than any,
From such as now they start the scene revisiting,
As a flock, twittering, rising, or overhead passing,
Borne hither, ere all eludes me, hurriedly,
A man, yet by these tears a little boy again,
Throwing myself on the sand, confronting the waves,
I, chanter of pains and joys, uniter of here and hereafter,
Taking all hints to use them, but swiftly leaping beyond
    them,
A reminiscence sing.

Once Paumanok,
When the lilac-scent was in the air and Fifth-month grass
    was growing,
Up this seashore in some briers,
Two feather'd guests from Alabama, two together,
And their nest, and four light-green eggs spotted with
    brown,
And every day the he-bird to and fro near at hand,
And every day the she-bird crouch'd on her nest, silent,
    with bright eyes,
And every day I, a curious boy, never too close, never
    disturbing them,
Cautiously peering, absorbing, translating.

Shine! shine! shine!
Pour down your warmth, great sun!
While we bask, we two together.

Two together!
Winds blow south, or winds blow north,
Day come white, or night come black,
Home, or rivers and mountains from home,
Singing all time, minding no time,
While we two keep together.

Till of a sudden,
May-be kill'd, unknown to her mate,
One forenoon the she-bird crouch'd not on the nest,
Nor return'd that afternoon, nor the next,
Nor ever appear'd again.

And thenceforward all summer in the sound of the sea,
And at night under the full of the moon in calmer weather,
Over the hoarse surging of the sea,
Or flitting from brier to brier by day,
I saw, I heard at intervals the remaining one, the he-bird,
The solitary guest from Alabama.

Blow! blow! blow!
Blow up sea-winds along Paumanok's shore;
I wait and I wait till you blow my mate to me.

Yes, when the stars glisten'd,
All night long on the prong of a moss-scallop'd stake,
Down almost amid the slapping waves,
Sat the lone singer wonderful causing tears.

He call'd on his mate,
He pour'd forth the meanings which I of all men know.

Yes my brother I know,
The rest might not, but I have treasur'd every note,
For more than once dimly down to the beach gliding,
Silent, avoiding the moonbeams, blending myself with the
    shadows,
Recalling now the obscure shapes, the echoes, the sounds
    and sights after their sorts,
The white arms out in the breakers tirelessly tossing,
I, with bare feet, a child, the wind wafting my hair,
Listen'd long and long.

Listen'd to keep, to sing, now translating the notes,
Following you my brother.

Soothe! soothe! soothe!
Close on its wave soothes the wave behind,
And again another behind embracing and lapping, every one
  close,
But my love soothes not me, not me.

Low hangs the moon, it rose late,
It is lagging—O I think it is heavy with love, with love.

O madly the sea pushes upon the land,
With love, with love.

O night! do I not see my love fluttering out among the
  breakers?
What is that little black thing I see there in the white?

Loud! loud! loud!
Loud I call to you, my love!
High and clear I shoot my voice over the waves,
Surely you must know who is here, is here,
You must know who I am, my love.

Low-hanging moon!
What is that dusky spot in your brown yellow?
O it is the shape, the shape of my mate!
O moon do not keep her from me any longer.

Land! land! O land!
Whichever way I turn, O I think you could give me my mate
  back again if you only would,
For I am almost sure I see her dimly whichever way I look.

O rising stars!

Perhaps the one I want so much will rise, will rise with some
    of you.

O throat! O trembling throat!
Sound clearer through the atmosphere!
Pierce the woods, the earth,
Somewhere listening to catch you must be the one I want.

Shake out carols!
Solitary here, the night's carols!
Carols of lonesome love! death's carols!
Carols under that lagging, yellow, waning moon!
O under that moon where she droops almost down into the sea!
O reckless despairing carols.

But soft! sink low!
Soft! let me just murmur,
And do you wait a moment you husky-nois'd sea,
For somewhere I believe I heard my mate responding to me,
So faint, I must be still, be still to listen,
But not altogether still, for then she might not come
    immediately to me.

Hither my love!
Here I am! here!
With this just-sustain'd note I announce myself to you,
This gentle call is for you my love, for you.

Do not be decoy'd elsewhere,
That is the whistle of the wind, it is not my voice,
That is the fluttering, the fluttering of the spray,
Those are the shadows of leaves.

O darkness! O in vain!
O I am very sick and sorrowful.

O brown halo in the sky near the moon, drooping upon the sea!

O troubled reflection in the sea!
O throat! O throbbing heart!
And I singing uselessly, uselessly all the night.

O past! O happy life! O songs of joy!
In the air, in the woods, over fields,
Loved! loved! loved! loved! loved!
But my mate no more, no more with me!
We two together no more.

The aria sinking,
All else continuing, the stars shining,
The winds blowing, the notes of the bird continuous
    echoing,
With angry moans the fierce old mother incessantly moaning,
On the sands of Paumanok's shore gray and rustling,
The yellow half-moon enlarged, sagging down, drooping,
    the face of the sea almost touching,
The boy ecstatic, with his bare feet the waves, with his
    hair the atmosphere dallying,
The love in the heart long pent, now loose, now at last
    tumultuously bursting,
The aria's meaning, the ears, the soul, swiftly depositing,
The strange tears down the cheeks coursing,
The colloquy there, the trio, each uttering,
The undertone, the savage old mother incessantly crying,
To the boy's soul's questions sullenly timing, some
    drown'd secret hissing,
To the outsetting bard.

Demon or bird! (said the boy's soul,)
Is it indeed toward your mate you sing? or is it really to me?
For I, that was a child, my tongue's use sleeping, now I have
    heard you,
Now in a moment I know what I am for, I awake,
And already a thousand singers, a thousand songs, clearer,
    louder and more sorrowful than yours,

A thousand warbling echoes have started to life within me,
    never to die.

O you singer solitary, singing by yourself, projecting me,
O solitary me listening, never more shall I cease
    perpetuating you,
Never more shall I escape, never more the reverberations,
Never more the cries of unsatisfied love be absent from me,
Never again leave me to be the peaceful child I was before
    what there in the night,
By the sea under the yellow and sagging moon,
The messenger there arous'd, the fire, the sweet hell
    within,
The unknown want, the destiny of me.

O give me the clew! (it lurks in the night here somewhere,)
O if I am to have so much, let me have more!

A word then, (for I will conquer it,)
The word final, superior to all,
Subtle, sent up—what is it?—I listen;
Are you whispering it, and have been all the time, you
    sea-waves?
Is that it from your liquid rims and wet sands?

Whereto answering, the sea,
Delaying not, hurrying not,
Whisper'd me through the night, and very plainly before
    daybreak,
Lisp'd to me the low and delicious word death,
And again death, death, death, death,
Hissing melodious, neither like the bird nor like my
    arous'd child's heart,
But edging near as privately for me rustling at my feet,
Creeping thence steadily up to my ears and laving me softly
    all over,

18 –

Death, death, death, death, death.

Which I do not forget,
But fuse the song of my dusky demon and brother,
That he sang to me in the moonlight on Paumanok's gray
    beach,
With the thousand responsive songs at random,
My own songs awaked from that hour,
And with them the key, the word up from the waves,
The word of the sweetest song and all songs,
That strong and delicious word which, creeping to my feet,
(Or like some old crone rocking the cradle, swathed in sweet
    garments, bending aside,)
The sea whisper'd me.

"You road I enter upon . . ."

From

SONG OF THE OPEN ROAD

Afoot and light-hearted I take to the open road,
Healthy, free, the world before me,
The long brown path before me leading wherever I choose.

Henceforth I ask not good-fortune, I myself am
    good-fortune,
Henceforth I whimper no more, postpone no more, need
    nothing,
Done with indoor complaints, libraries, querulous
    criticisms,
Strong and content I travel the open road.

The earth, that is sufficient,
I do not want the constellations any nearer,
I know they are very well where they are,
I know they suffice for those who belong to them.

(Still here I carry my old delicious burdens,
I carry them, men and women, I carry them with me
    wherever I go,
I swear it is impossible for me to get rid of them,
I am fill'd with them, and I will fill them in return.)

You road I enter upon and look around, I believe you are
    not all that is here,
I believe that much unseen is also here.

ON JOURNEYS THROUGH THE STATES

On journeys through the States we start,
(Ay through the world, urged by these songs,
Sailing henceforth to every land, to every sea,)
We willing learners of all, teachers of all, and lovers of all.

We have watch'd the seasons dispensing themselves and
   passing on,
And have said, Why should not a man or woman do as much
   as the seasons, and effuse as much?

We dwell a while in every city and town,
We pass through Kanada, the North-east, the vast valley of
   the Mississippi, and the Southern States,
We confer on equal terms with each of the States,
We make trial of ourselves and invite men and women to
   hear,
We say to ourselves, Remember, fear not, be candid,
   promulge the body and the soul,
Dwell a while and pass on, be copious, temperate, chaste,
   magnetic,
And what you effuse may then return as the seasons return,
And may be just as much as the seasons.

TO RICH GIVERS

What you give me I cheerfully accept,
A little sustenance, a hut and garden, a little money, as I
  rendezvous with my poems,
A traveler's lodging and breakfast as I journey through the
  States,—why should I be ashamed to own such gifts? why
  to advertise for them?
For I myself am not one who bestows nothing upon man
  and woman,
For I bestow upon any man or woman the entrance to all
  the gifts of the universe.

LOCATIONS AND TIMES

Locations and times—what is it in me that meets them all,
  whenever and wherever, and makes me at home?
Forms, colors, densities, odors—what is it in me that
  corresponds with them?

EXCELSIOR

Who has gone farthest? for I would go farther,
And who has been just? for I would be the most just person
   of the earth,
And who most cautious? for I would be more cautious,
And who has been happiest? O I think it is I—I think no one
   was ever happier than I,
And who has lavish'd all? for I lavish constantly the best I
   have,
And who proudest? for I think I have reason to be the
   proudest son alive—for I am the son of the brawny and
   tall-topt city,
And who has been bold and true? for I would be the
   boldest and truest being of the universe,
And who benevolent? for I would show more benevolence
   than all the rest,
And who has receiv'd the love of the most friends? for I
   know what it is to receive the passionate love of many
   friends,
And who possesses a perfect and enamour'd body? for I do
   not believe any one possesses a more perfect or
   enamour'd body than mine,
And who thinks the amplest thoughts? for I would
   surround those thoughts,
And who has made hymns fit for the earth? for I am mad
   with devouring ecstasy to make joyous hymns for the
   whole earth.

From

GREAT ARE THE MYTHS

Great is To-day, and beautiful,
It is good to live in this age—there never was any better . . .

Great are Yourself and Myself,
We are just as good and bad as the oldest and youngest
   or any,
What the best and worst did, we could do,
What they felt, do not we feel it in ourselves?
What they wished, do we not wish the same?

Great is Youth—equally great is Old Age—great are the
   Day and Night;
Great is Wealth—great is Poverty—great is Expression—
   great is Silence.

Youth, large, lusty, loving—Youth, full of grace, force,
   fascination,
Do you know that Old Age may come after you,
   with equal grace, force, fascination?

From

STARTING FROM PAUMANOK

Victory, union, faith, identity, time,
The indissoluble compacts, riches, mystery,
Eternal progress, the kosmos, and the modern reports.

This then is life,
Here is what has come to the surface after so many throes
   and convulsions.

How curious! how real!
Underfoot the divine soil, overhead the sun.

From

SONG OF MYSELF

I have heard what the talkers were talking, the talk of the
   beginning and the end,
But I do not talk of the beginning or the end.

There was never any more inception than there is now,
Nor any more youth or age than there is now,
And will never be any more perfection than there is now,
Nor any more heaven or hell than there is now.

From

SONG OF MYSELF

You sea! I resign myself to you also—I guess what you
    mean,
I behold from the beach your crooked inviting fingers,
I believe you refuse to go back without feeling of me,
We must have a turn together, I undress, hurry me out of
    sight of the land,
Cushion me soft, rock me in billowy drowse,
Dash me with amorous wet, I can repay you.

Sea of stretch'd ground-swells,
Sea breathing broad and convulsive breaths,
Sea of the brine of life and of unshovell'd yet
    always-ready graves,
Howler and scooper of storms, capricious and dainty sea,
I am integral with you, I too am of one phase and of all
    phases.

From

SONG OF MYSELF

I think I could turn and live with animals, they are so placid
    and self-contain'd,
I stand and look at them long and long.

They do not sweat and whine about their condition,
They do not lie awake in the dark and weep for their sins,
They do not make me sick discussing their duty to God,
Not one is dissatisfied, not one is demented with the mania
    of owning things,
Not one kneels to another, nor to his kind that lived
    thousands of years ago,
Not one is respectable or unhappy over the whole earth.

HAST NEVER COME TO
THEE AN HOUR

Hast never come to thee an hour,
A sudden gleam divine, precipitating, bursting all these
    bubbles, fashions, wealth?
These eager business aims—books, politics, art, amours,
To utter nothingness?

29 –

STRONGER LESSONS

Have you learn'd lessons only of those who admired you,
   and were tender with you, and stood aside for you?
Have you not learn'd great lessons from those who reject
   you, and brace themselves against you? or who treat you
   with contempt, or dispute the passage with you?

WHEN I HEARD THE LEARN'D ASTRONOMER

When I heard the learn'd astronomer,
When the proofs, the figures, were ranged in columns before
   me,
When I was shown the charts and diagrams, to add, divide,
   and measure them,
When I sitting heard the astronomer where he lectured with
   much applause in the lecture-room,
How soon unaccountable I became tired and sick,
Till rising and gliding out I wander'd off by myself,
In the mystical moist night-air, and from time to time,
Look'd up in perfect silence at the stars.

From

SONG OF THE ANSWERER

All this time and at all times wait the words of true poems,
The words of true poems do not merely please,
The true poets are not followers of beauty but the august
    masters of beauty;
The greatness of sons is the exuding of the greatness of
    mothers and fathers,
The words of true poems are the tuft and final applause of
    science.

Divine instinct, breadth of vision, the law of reason, health,
    rudeness of body, withdrawnness,
Gayety, sun-tan, air-sweetness, such are some of the words
    of poems.

The sailor and traveler underlie the maker of poems, the
    Answerer,
The builder, geometer, chemist, anatomist, phrenologist,
    artist, all these underlie the maker of poems, the
    Answerer.

The words of the true poems give you more than poems,
They give you to form for yourself poems, religions, politics,
    war, peace, behavior, histories, essays, daily life, and
    every thing else,
They balance ranks, colors, races, creeds, and the sexes,
They do not seek beauty, they are sought,
Forever touching them or close upon them follows beauty,
    longing, fain, love-sick.

"I mourned, and yet shall mourn . . ."

From

SONG OF MYSELF

The runaway slave came to my house and stopt outside,
I heard his motions crackling the twigs of the woodpile,
Through the swung half-door of the kitchen I saw him
    limpsy and weak,
And went where he sat on a log and led him in and assured
    him,
And brought water and fill'd a tub for his sweated body and
    bruis'd feet,
And gave him a room that enter'd from my own, and gave
    him some coarse clean clothes,
And remember perfectly well his revolving eyes and his
    awkwardness,
And remember putting plasters on the galls of his neck
    and ankles;
He staid with me a week before he was recuperated and
    pass'd north,
I had him sit next me at table, my fire-lock lean'd in the
    corner.

THOUGHT

Of obedience, faith, adhesiveness;
As I stand aloof and look there is to me something
    profoundly affecting in large masses of men following the
    lead of those who do not believe in men.

O TAN-FACED PRAIRIE-BOY

O tan-faced prairie-boy,
Before you came to camp came many a welcome gift,
Praises and presents came and nourishing food, till at last
    among the recruits,
You came, taciturn, with nothing to give—we but look'd on
    each other,
When lo! more than all the gifts of the world you gave me.

COME UP FROM THE
FIELDS FATHER

Come up from the fields father, here's a letter from our
    Pete,
And come to the front door mother, here's a letter from thy
    dear son.

Lo, 'tis autumn,
Lo, where the trees, deeper green, yellower and redder,
Cool and sweeten Ohio's villages with leaves fluttering in
    the moderate wind,
Where apples ripe in the orchard hang and grapes on the
    trellis'd vines,
(Smell you the smell of the grapes on the vines?
Smell you the buckwheat where the bees were lately
    buzzing?)

Above all, lo, the sky so calm, so transparent after the rain,
    and with wondrous clouds,

Below too, all calm, all vital and beautiful, and the farm
  prospers well.

Down in the fields all prospers well,
But now from the fields come father, come at the daughter's
  call,
And come to the entry mother, to the front door come right
  away.

Fast as she can she hurries, something ominous, her steps
  trembling,
She does not tarry to smooth her hair nor adjust her cap.

Open the envelope quickly,
O this is not our son's writing, yet his name is sign'd,
O a strange hand writes for our dear son, O stricken
  mother's soul!
All swims before her eyes, flashes with black, she catches the
  main words only,
Sentences broken, *gunshot wound in the breast, cavalry
  skirmish, taken to hospital,*
At present low, but will soon be better.

Ah now the single figure to me,
Amid all teeming and wealthy Ohio with all its cities and
  farms,
Sickly white in the face and dull in the head, very faint,
By the jamb of a door leans.

Grieve not so, dear mother, (the just-grown daughter speaks
  through her sobs,
The little sisters huddle around speechless and dismay'd,)
See, dearest mother, the letter says Pete will soon be better.

Alas poor boy, he will never be better, (nor may-be needs
  to be better, that brave and simple soul,)

While they stand at home at the door he is dead already,
The only son is dead.

But the mother needs to be better,
She with thin form presently drest in black,
By day her meals untouch'd, then at night fitfully sleeping,
    often waking,
In the midnight waking, weeping, longing with one deep
    longing,
O that she might withdraw unnoticed, silent from life escape
    and withdraw,
To follow, to seek, to be with her dear dead son.

GLIDING O'ER ALL

Gliding o'er all, through all,
Through Nature, Time, and Space,
As a ship on the waters advancing,
The voyage of the soul—not life alone,
Death, many deaths I'll sing.

WHEN LILACS LAST IN THE DOORYARD BLOOM'D

1

When lilacs last in the dooryard bloom'd,
And the great star early droop'd in the western sky in the
  night,
I mourn'd, and yet shall mourn with ever-returning spring.

Ever-returning spring, trinity sure to me you bring,
Lilac blooming perennial and drooping star in the west,
And thought of him I love.

2

O powerful western fallen star!
O shades of night—O moody, tearful night!
O great star disappear'd—O the black murk that hides the
  star!
O cruel hands that hold me powerless—O helpless soul of
  me!
O harsh surrounding cloud that will not free my soul.

3

In the dooryard fronting an old farm-house near the
  white-wash'd palings,
Stands the lilac-bush tall-growing with heart-shaped leaves
  of rich green,
With many a pointed blossom rising delicate, with the
  perfume strong I love,
With every leaf a miracle—and from this bush in the
  dooryard,
With delicate-color'd blossoms and heart-shaped leaves of
  rich green,
A sprig with its flower I break.

4

In the swamp in secluded recesses,
A shy and hidden bird is warbling a song.

Solitary the thrush,
The hermit withdrawn to himself, avoiding the settlements,
Sings by himself a song.

Song of the bleeding throat,
Death's outlet song of life, (for well dear brother I know,
If thou wast not granted to sing thou would'st surely die.)

5

Over the breast of the spring, the land, amid cities,
Amid lanes and through old woods, where lately the violets
  peep'd from the ground, spotting the gray debris,
Amid the grass in the fields each side of the lanes, passing
  the endless grass,
Passing the yellow-spear'd wheat, every grain from its
  shroud in the dark-brown fields uprisen,
Passing the apple-tree blows of white and pink in the
  orchards,

Carrying a corpse to where it shall rest in the grave,
Night and day journeys a coffin.

6

Coffin that passes through lanes and streets,
Through day and night with the great cloud darkening the
    land,
With the pomp of the inloop'd flags with the cities draped
    in black,
With the show of the States themselves as of crape-veil'd
    women standing,
With processions long and winding and the flambeaus of the
    night,
With the countless torches lit, with the silent sea of faces
    and the unbared heads,
With the waiting depot, the arriving coffin, and the sombre
    faces,
With dirges through the night, with the thousand voices
    rising strong and solemn,
With all the mournful voices of the dirges pour'd around the
    coffin,
The dim-lit churches and the shuddering organs—where
    amid these you journey,
With the tolling tolling bells' perpetual clang,
Here, coffin that slowly passes,
I give you my sprig of lilac.

7

(Nor for you, for one alone,
Blossoms and branches green to coffins all I bring,
For fresh as the morning, thus would I chant a song for you
    O sane and sacred death.

All over bouquets of roses,
O death, I cover you over with roses and early lilies,
But mostly and now the lilac that blooms the first,

42 –

Copious I break, I break the sprigs from the bushes,
With loaded arms I come, pouring for you,
For you and the coffins all of you O death.)

8

O western orb sailing the heaven,
Now I know what you must have meant as a month since I
    walk'd,
As I walk'd in silence the transparent shadowy night,
As I saw you had something to tell as you bent to me night
    after night,
As you droop'd from the sky low down as if to my side,
    (while the other stars all look'd on,)
As we wander'd together the solemn night, (for something I
    know not what kept me from sleep,)
As the night advanced, and I saw on the rim of the west how
    full you were of woe,
As I stood on the rising ground in the breeze in the cool
    transparent night,
As I watch'd where you pass'd and was lost in the
    netherward black of the night,
As my soul in its trouble dissatisfied sank, as where you sad
    orb,
Concluded, dropt in the night, and was gone.

9

Sing on there in the swamp,
O singer bashful and tender, I hear your notes, I hear your
    call,
I hear, I come presently, I understand you,
But a moment I linger, for the lustrous star has detain'd me,
The star my departing comrade holds and detains me.

10

O how shall I warble myself for the dead one there I loved?
And how shall I deck my song for the large sweet soul that
    has gone?
And what shall my perfume be for the grave of him I love?

Sea-winds blown from east and west,
Blown from the Eastern sea and blown from the Western
    sea, till there on the prairies meeting,
These and with these and the breath of my chant,
I'll perfume the grave of him I love.

11

O what shall I hang on the chamber walls?
And what shall the pictures be that I hang on the walls,
To adorn the burial-house of him I love?

Pictures of growing spring and farms and homes,
With the Fourth-month eve at sundown, and the gray smoke
    lucid and bright,
With floods of the yellow gold of the gorgeous, indolent,
    sinking sun, burning, expanding the air,
With the fresh sweet herbage under foot, and the pale
    green leaves of the trees prolific,
In the distance the flowing glaze, the breast of the river, with
    a wind-dapple here and there,
With ranging hills on the banks, with many a line against the
    sky, and shadows,

And the city at hand with dwellings so dense, and stacks of
    chimneys,
And all the scenes of life and the workshops, and the
    workmen homeward returning.

12

Lo, body and soul—this land,
My own Manhattan with spires, and the sparkling and
    hurrying tides, and the ships,
The varied and ample land, the South and the North in the
    light, Ohio's shores and flashing Missouri,
And ever the far-spreading prairies cover'd with grass and
    corn.

Lo, the most excellent sun so calm and haughty,
The violet and purple morn with just-felt breezes,
The gentle soft-born measureless light,
The miracle spreading bathing all, the fulfill'd noon,
The coming eve delicious, the welcome night and the stars,
Over my cities shining all, enveloping man and land.

13

Sing on, sing on you gray-brown bird,
Sing from the swamps, the recesses, pour your chant from
    the bushes,
Limitless out of the dusk, out of the cedars and pines.

Sing on dearest brother, warble your reedy song,
Loud human song, with voice of uttermost woe.

O liquid and free and tender!
O wild and loose to my soul—O wondrous singer!
You only I hear—yet the star holds me, (but will soon
    depart,)
Yet the lilac with mastering odor holds me.

14

Now while I sat in the day and look'd forth,
In the close of the day with its light and the fields of spring,
    and the farmers preparing their crops,
In the large unconscious scenery of my land with its lakes
    and forests,
In the heavenly aerial beauty, (after the perturb'd winds and
    the storms,)
Under the arching heavens of the afternoon swift passing,
    and the voices of children and women,
The many-moving sea-tides, and I saw the ships how they
    sail'd,
And the summer approaching with richness, and the fields
    all busy with labor,
And the infinite separate houses, how they all went on, each
    with its meals and minutia of daily usages,
And the streets how their throbbings throbb'd, and the
    cities pent—lo, then and there,
Falling upon them all and among them all, enveloping me
    with the rest,
Appear'd the cloud, appear'd the long black trail,
And I knew death, its thought, and the sacred knowledge of
    death.

Then with the knowledge of death as walking one side of me,
And the thought of death close-walking the other side of me,
And I in the middle as with companions, and as holding the
    hands of companions,
I fled forth to the hiding receiving night that talks not,
Down to the shores of the water, the path by the swamp in
    the dimness,
To the solemn shadowy cedars and ghostly pines so still.

And the singer so shy to the rest receiv'd me,
The gray-brown bird I know receiv'd us comrades three,
And he sang the carol of death, and a verse for him I love.

From deep secluded recesses,
From the fragrant cedars and the ghostly pines so still,
Came the carol of the bird.

And the charm of the carol rapt me,
As I held as if by their hands my comrades in the night,
And the voice of my spirit tallied the song of the bird.

Come lovely and soothing death,
Undulate round the world, serenely arriving, arriving,
In the day, in the night, to all, to each,
Sooner or later delicate death.

Prais'd be the fathomless universe,
For life and joy, and for objects and knowledge curious,
And for love, sweet love—but praise! praise! praise!
For the sure-enwinding arms of cool-enfolding death.

Dark mother always gliding near with soft feet,
Have none chanted for thee a chant of fullest welcome?
Then I chant it for thee, I glorify thee above all,
I bring thee a song that when thou must indeed come, come
  unfalteringly.

Approach strong deliveress,
When it is so, when thou hast taken them I joyously sing the
  dead,
Lost in the loving floating ocean of thee,
Laved in the flood of thy bliss O death.

From me to thee glad serenades,
Dances for thee I propose saluting thee, adornments and
  feastings for thee,
And the sights of the open landscape and the high-spread sky
  are fitting,
And life and the fields, and the huge and thoughtful night.

The night in silence under many a star,
The ocean shore and the husky whispering wave whose voice I
   know,
And the soul turning to thee O vast and well-veil'd death,
And the body gratefully nestling close to thee.

Over the tree-tops I float thee a song,
Over the rising and sinking waves, over the myriad fields and
   the prairies wide,
Over the dense-pack'd cities all and the teeming wharves and
   ways,
I float this carol with joy, with joy to thee O death.

15

To the tally of my soul,
Loud and strong kept up the gray-brown bird,
With pure deliberate notes spreading filling the night.

Loud in the pines and cedars dim,
Clear in the freshness moist and the swamp-perfume,
And I with my comrades there in the night.

While my sight that was bound in my eyes unclosed,
As to long panoramas of visions.

And I saw askant the armies,
I saw as in noiseless dreams hundreds of battle-flags,
Borne through the smoke of the battles and pierc'd with
   missiles I saw them,
And carried hither and yon through the smoke, and torn
   and bloody,
And at last but a few shreds left on the staffs, (and all in
   silence,)
And the staffs all splinter'd and broken.

I saw battle-corpses, myriads of them,
And the white skeletons of young men, I saw them,

I saw the debris and debris of all the slain soldiers of the
    war,
But I saw they were not as was thought,
They themselves were fully at rest, they suffer'd not,
The living remain'd and suffer'd, the mother suffer'd,
And the wife and the child and the musing comrade suffer'd,
And the armies that remain'd suffer'd.

16

Passing the visions, passing the night,
Passing, unloosing the hold of my comrades' hands,
Passing the song of the hermit bird and the tallying song of
    my soul,
Victorious song, death's outlet song, yet varying
    ever-altering song,
As low and wailing, yet clear the notes, rising and falling,
    flooding the night,
Sadly sinking and fainting, as warning and warning, and yet
    again bursting with joy,
Covering the earth and filling the spread of the heaven,
As that powerful psalm in the night I heard from recesses,
Passing, I leave thee lilac with heart-shaped leaves,
I leave thee there in the door-yard, blooming, returning
    with spring.

I cease from my song for thee,
From my gaze on thee in the west, fronting the west,
    communing with thee,
O comrade lustrous with silver face in the night.

Yet each to keep and all, retrievements out of the night,
The song, the wondrous chant of the gray-brown bird,
And the tallying chant, the echo arous'd in my soul,
With the lustrous and drooping star with the countenance
    full of woe,
With the holders holding my hand nearing the call of the
    bird,

49 —

Comrades mine and I in the midst, and their memory ever
    to keep, for the dead I loved so well,
For the sweetest, wisest soul of all my days and lands—and
    this for his dear sake,
Lilac and star and bird twined with the chant of my soul,
There in the fragrant pines and the cedars dusk and dim.

I DREAM'D IN A DREAM

I dream'd in a dream I saw a city invincible to the attacks
   of the whole of the rest of the earth,
I dream'd that was the new city of Friends,
Nothing was greater there than the quality of robust love, it
   led the rest,
It was seen every hour in the actions of the men of that city,
And in all their looks and words.

"I am the poet of the Body and I am the poet of the Soul . . ."

From

SONG OF MYSELF

I am the poet of the Body and I am the poet of the Soul,
The pleasures of heaven are with me and the pains of hell
   are with me,
The first I graft and increase upon myself, the latter I
   translate into a new tongue.

I am the poet of the woman the same as the man,
And I say it is as great to be a woman as to be a man,
And I say there is nothing greater than the mother of men.

MOTHER AND BABE

I see the sleeping babe nestling the breast of its mother,
The sleeping mother and babe—hush'd, I study them long
   and long.

BEAUTIFUL WOMEN

Women sit or move to and fro, some old, some young,
The young are beautiful—but the old are more beautiful
    than the young.

From

SAYS

1

I say whatever tastes sweet to the most perfect person, that
    is finally right.

2

I say nourish a great intellect, a great brain;
If I have said anything to the contrary, I hereby retract it.

3

I say man shall not hold property in man;
I say the least developed person on earth is just as important
    and sacred to himself or herself, as the most developed
    person is to himself or herself.

TO YOU

Stranger, if you passing meet me and desire to speak to me,
    why should you not speak to me?
And why should I not speak to you?

From

STARTING FROM PAUMANOK

What do you seek so pensive and silent?
What do you need camerado?
Dear son do you think it is love?

Listen dear son—listen America, daughter or son,
It is a painful thing to love a man or woman to excess, and
  yet it satisfies, it is great,
But there is something else very great, it makes the whole
  coincide,
It, magnificent, beyond materials, with continuous hands
  sweeps and provides for all.

POETS TO COME

Poets to come! orators, singers, musicians to come!
Not to-day is to justify me and answer what I am for,
But you, a new brood, native, athletic, continental, greater
  than before known,
Arouse! for you must justify me.

I myself but write one or two indicative words for the future,
I but advance a moment only to wheel and hurry back in the
  darkness.

I am a man who, sauntering along without fully stopping,
  turns a casual look upon you and then averts his face,
Leaving it to you to prove and define it,
Expecting the main things from you.

WHAT AM I AFTER ALL

What am I after all but a child, pleas'd with the sound of
    my own name? repeating it over and over;
I stand apart to hear—it never tires me.

To you your name also;
Did you think there was nothing but two or three
    pronunciations in the sound of your name?

TO SOAR IN FREEDOM AND IN FULLNESS OF POWER

I have not so much emulated the birds that musically sing,
I have abandon'd myself to flights, broad circles.
The hawk, the seagull, have far more possess'd me than the
    canary or mocking-bird,
I have not felt to warble and trill, however sweetly,
I have felt to soar in freedom and in the fullness of power,
    joy, volition.

"So long—*And I hope we shall meet again.*"

GOOD-BYE MY FANCY!

Good-bye my Fancy!
Farewell dear mate, dear love!
I'm going away, I know not where,
Or to what fortune, or whether I may ever see you again,
So Good-bye my Fancy.

Now for my last—let me look back a moment;
The slower fainter ticking of the clock is in me,
Exit, nightfall, and soon the heart-thud stopping.

Long have we lived, joy'd, caress'd together;
Delightful!—now separation—Good-bye my Fancy.

Yet let me not be too hasty,
Long indeed have we lived, slept, filter'd, become really
   blended into one;
Then if we die we die together, (yes, we'll remain one,)
If we go anywhere we'll go together to meet what happens,
May-be we'll be better off and blither, and learn something,
May-be it is yourself now really ushering me to the true
   songs, (who knows?)
May-be it is you the mortal knob really undoing, turning—
   so now finally,
Good-bye—and hail! my Fancy.

TO GET THE FINAL LILT
OF SONGS

To get the final lilt of songs,
To penetrate the inmost lore of poets—to know the mighty
    ones,
Job, Homer, Eschylus, Dante, Shakspere, Tennyson,
    Emerson;
To diagnose the shifting-delicate tints of love and pride and
    doubt—to truly understand,
To encompass these, the last keen faculty and
    entrance-price,
Old age, and what it brings from all its past experiences.

AFTER THE DAZZLE OF DAY

After the dazzle of day is gone,
Only the dark, dark night shows to my eyes the stars;
After the clangor of organ majestic, or chorus, or perfect
    band,
Silent, athwart my soul, moves the symphony true.

A CLEAR MIDNIGHT

This is thy hour O Soul, thy free flight into the wordless,
Away from books, away from art, the day erased, the lesson
    done,
Thee fully forth emerging, silent, gazing, pondering the
    themes thou lovest best,
Night, sleep, death and the stars.

TO OLD AGE

I see in you the estuary that enlarges and spreads itself
    grandly as it pours in the great sea.

YEAR THAT TREMBLED AND REEL'D BENEATH ME

Year that trembled and reel'd beneath me!
Your summer wind was warm enough, yet the air I breathed
    froze me,
A thick gloom fell through the sunshine and darken'd me,
Must I change my triumphant songs? said I to myself,
Must I indeed learn to chant the cold dirges of the baffled?
And sullen hymns of defeat?

WHEN I READ THE BOOK

When I read the book, the biography famous,
And is this then (said I) what the author calls a man's life?
And so will some one when I am dead and gone write my
  life?
(As if any man really knew aught of my life,
Why even I myself I often think how little or nothing of
  my real life,
Only a few hints, a few diffused faint clews and indirections
I seek for my own use to trace out here.)

ONE THOUGHT EVER AT THE FORE

One thought ever at the fore—
That in the Divine Ship, the World, breasting Time and
  Space,
All Peoples of the globe together sail, sail the same voyage,
  are bound to the same destination.

QUERIES TO MY SEVENTIETH YEAR

Approaching, nearing, curious,
Thou dim, uncertain spectre—bringest thou life or death?
Strength, weakness, blindness, more paralysis and heavier?
Or placid skies and sun? Wilt stir the waters yet?
Or haply cut me short for good? Or leave me here as now,
Dull, parrot-like and old, with crack'd voice harping,
    screeching?

MY 71ST YEAR

After surmounting three-score and ten,
With all their chances, changes, losses, sorrows,
My parents' deaths, the vagaries of my life, the many tearing
    passions of me, the war of '63 and '64,
As some old broken soldier, after a long, hot, wearying
    march, or haply after battle,
To-day at twilight, hobbling, answering company roll-call,
    Here, with vital voice,
Reporting yet, saluting yet the Officer over all.

MEMORIES

How sweet the silent backward tracings!
The wanderings as in dreams—the meditation of old times
    resumed—their loves, joys, persons, voyages.

NO LABOR-SAVING MACHINE

No labor-saving machine,
Nor discovery have I made,
Nor will I be able to leave behind me any wealthy bequest
    to found a hospital or library,
Nor reminiscence of any deed of courage for America,
Nor literary success nor intellect, nor book for the
    book-shelf,
But a few carols vibrating through the air I leave,
For comrades and lovers.

MY LEGACY

The business man the acquirer vast,
After assiduous years surveying results, preparing for
   departure,
Devises houses and lands to his children, bequeaths stocks,
   goods, funds for a school or hospital,
Leaves money to certain companions to buy tokens,
   souvenirs of gems and gold.

But I, my life surveying, closing,
With nothing to show to devise from its idle years,
Nor houses nor lands, nor tokens of gems or gold for my
   friends,
Yet certain remembrances of the war for you, and after you,
And little souvenirs of camps and soldiers, with my love,
I bind together and bequeath in this bundle of songs.

NOW LIFT ME CLOSE

Now lift me close to your face till I whisper,
What you are holding is in reality no book, nor part of
  a book;
It is a man, flush'd and full blooded—it is I—*So long!*—
We must separate awhile—Here! take from my lips this kiss;
Whoever you are, I give it especially to you;
So long!—And I hope we shall meet again.

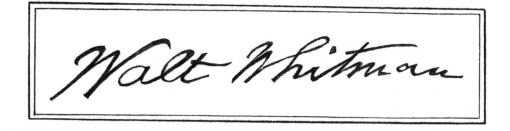

INDEX OF TITLES

INDEX OF FIRST LINES

I hear America singing, the varied carols I hear,   9

I say whatever tastes sweet to the most perfect person,
   that is finally right.   *55*

I see in you the estuary that enlarges and spreads itself
   grandly as it pours in the great sea.   *63*

I see the sleeping babe nestling the breast of its
   mother,   *54*

I think I could turn and live with animals, they are so
   placid and self-contained,   *29*

I was asking for something specific and perfect for my
   city,   *7*

Locations and times—what is it in me that meets them all,
   whenever and wherever, and makes me at home?   *24*

No labor-saving machine,   *66*

Now lift me close to your face till I whisper,   *68*

O take my hand Walt Whitman!   *xv*

O tan-faced prairie-boy,   *35*

Of obedience, faith, adhesiveness;   *35*

On journeys through the States we start,   *23*

One thought ever at the fore—   *64*

Out of the cradle endlessly rocking,   *12*

Poets to come! orators, singers, musicians to come!   *56*

See, steamers steaming through my poems,   *10*

Shut not your doors to me proud libraries,   *4*

Starting from fish-shape Paumanok where I was
   born,   *6*

Stranger, if you passing meet me and desire to speak to
   me, why should you not speak to me?   *55*

72 –

The business man the acquirer vast,   *67*
The runaway slave came to my house and stopt
  outside,   *34*
This is thy hour O Soul, thy free flight into the
  wordless,   *62*
Thou reader throbbest life and pride and love the same
  as I,   *5*
To get the final lilt of songs,   *61*

Victory, union, faith, identity, time,   *27*

What am I after all but a child, pleas'd with the sound of
  my own name? repeating it over and over;   *57*
What do you seek so pensive and silent?   *56*
What you give me I cheerfully accept,   *24*
When I heard the learn'd astronomer,   *30*
When I read the book, the biography famous,   *64*
When lilacs last in the dooryard bloom'd,   *40*
Who has gone farthest? for I would go farther,   *25*
Women sit or move to and fro, some old, some
  young,   *55*

Year that trembled and reel'd beneath me!   *63*
You sea! I resign myself to you also—I guess what you
  mean,   *28*

WHITMAN, WALT   02/03/89

$15.95

DATE			

NORTHPORT PUBLIC LIBRARY
NORTHPORT, NEW YORK

© THE BAKER & TAYLOR CO.